WHSmith

Revise
English

KS1: YEAR 2
Book 1

Age 6–7

Louis Fidge

The *WHS Revise* series

The *WHS Revise* books enable you to help your child revise and practise important skills taught in school. These skills form part of the National Curriculum and will help your child to improve his or her Maths and English.

Testing in schools

During their time at school all children will undergo a variety of tests. Regular testing is a feature of all schools. It is carried out:

● *informally* – in everyday classroom activities your child's teacher is continually assessing and observing your child's performance in a general way
● *formally* – more regular formal testing helps the teacher check your child's progress in specific areas.

Testing is important because:

● it provides evidence of your child's achievement and progress
● it helps the teacher decide which skills to focus on with your child
● it helps compare how different children are progressing.

The importance of revision

Regular revision is important to ensure your child remembers and practises skills he or she has been taught. These books will help your child revise and test his or her knowledge of some of the things he or she will be expected to know. They will help you prepare your child to be in a better position to face tests in school with confidence.

How to use this book

Units

This book is divided into twenty units, each focusing on one key skill. Each unit begins with a **Remember** section, which introduces and revises essential information about the particular skill covered. If possible, read and discuss this with your child to ensure he or she understands it.

This is followed by a **Have a go** section, which contains a number of activities to help your child revise the topic thoroughly and use the skill effectively. Usually, your child should be able to undertake these activities fairly independently.

Revision tests

There are two revision tests in this book (pages 24–27). These test the skills covered in the preceding units and assess your child's progress and understanding. They can be marked by you or by your child. Your child should fill in his or her test score for each test in the space provided. This will provide a visual record of your child's progress and an instant sense of confidence and achievement.

Parents' notes

The parents' notes (on pages 28–29) provide you with brief information on each skill and explain why it is important.

Answers

Answers to the unit questions and tests may be found on pages 30–32.

First published 2007
exclusively for WHSmith by
Hodder Education, part of Hachette Livre UK,
338 Euston Road
London
NW1 3BH

Impression number   10 9 8 7 6 5 4 3 2
Year   2008

A CIP record for this book is available from the British Library.

Cover illustration by Sally Newton Illustrations

Typeset by Fakenham Photosetting Limited, Fakenham, Norfolk

ISBN 978 034 094 2659

Printed and bound in Italy.

Contents

Remember

There are **five vowels** in the alphabet. They are **a**, **e**, **i**, **o** and **u**.

All the other letters are **consonants**.

Most words have **at least one vowel**.

a b c d e f g h i j k l m n o p q r s t u v w x y z

Have a go

1 Read the words. Underline the vowel in each word.

hat	bed	pin	cot	but
sip	fat	sun	get	pot
hug	net	lap	fog	bin

2 Put in the missing vowel in each word.

a	b	c	d	e
fr__g	dr__m	s__ck	l__g	k__ss

f	g	h	i	j
r__g	h__ll	n__st	m__p	b__g

Remember

When we spell words we have to build them up from **phonemes** (**letters** or **groups of letters**).

c + a + t   d + o + g

cat   dog

Have a go

1 Do these word sums. One is done for you.

a m + a + p = __map__

b h + e + n = _____

c s + i + x = _____

d c + o + t = _____

e h + u + t = _____

f z + i + p = _____

g p + e + g = _____

h c + a + p = _____

i l + o + g = _____

j m + u + g = _____

2 Use the words you have made. Write the correct word under each picture.

a	b	c	d	e
			6	
_____	_____	_____	_____	_____

f	g	h	i	j
_____	_____	_____	_____	_____

Unit 3: Rhyming words

Remember

We have to **listen** carefully to **hear** words that **rhyme**.

Sometimes rhyming words have the **same letters** at the **end**.

m**oon**

sp**oon**

Have a go

Join up the pairs of rhyming words.

Write the words here.
Read the words.

hill	tray
lick	cost
stay	fill
bite	greet
lost	stick
cry	white
meet	throw
rain	groan
slow	try
moan	drain

hill   fill

 **Remember**

Every sentence must **make sense**.

The monkey ate a  bath.
 banana.

The monkey ate a banana.

 **Have a go**

Choose the best ending for each sentence. One has been done for you.

a A car has four wheels.
 four hands.

__A car has four wheels.__

b The mouse roared.
 squeaked.

_____

c Tom drank an apple.
 a cup of tea.

_____

d The girl read the bus.
 the book.

_____

e A squirrel ran up the tree.
 above the tree.

_____

f An apple has lots of pips.
 lots of pops.

_____

g The lion roared.
 reared.

_____

Unit 5: Capital letters and full stops

Remember

Every sentence must **begin** with a **capital letter**.

The horse is in a field.

Many sentences **end** with a **full stop**.

Have a go

Write these sentences correctly. They make a story.

a   claire ran home from school

_____

b   she felt very hungry

_____

c   claire went into the kitchen

_____

d   she made some cheese sandwiches

_____

e   then she put some cakes on the table

_____

f   next claire put some crisps in a dish

_____

g   after this she made a drink

_____

h   when everything was ready claire had her tea

_____

Unit 6: Checking up on nouns

Remember

Some words **name** things. They are called **nouns**, or **naming words**.

apple    fish    hill

Have a go

1 Write the correct noun in each gap.

> aeroplane   boat   fire engine   submarine   train   ambulance

a   A _____ floats on water.

b   An _____ takes sick people to hospital.

c   An _____ flies in the sky.

d   A _____ carries firefighters to a fire.

e   A _____ is a ship that can travel underwater.

f   A _____ runs on rails and carries people.

2 Fill each gap with a suitable noun.

a   Children are taught in a _____.

b   A _____ is a tool for hitting things like nails.

c   You turn on a _____ to get water.

d   We need _____ to buy things.

e   A _____ is used to cut food when we eat.

f   You can see through a _____ because it is made of glass.

Remember

Sentences we write should **make sense**.
The beginning and ending of these sentences
have got mixed up.

Fish can ⟶ fly. ⟶ Birds can fly.

Birds can ⟶ swim. ⟶ Fish can swim.

Have a go

1 Match up the beginning and ending of each sentence.

Write the sentences correctly.

Snakes	swim.	_____
Birds	gallop.	_____
Sharks	slither. ⟶	Snakes slither.
Butterflies	hop.	_____
Horses	fly.	_____
Frogs	flutter.	_____

2 Match up the beginning and ending of each sentence.

Write each sentence and punctuate it correctly.

you drink	are very muddy	_____
the butterfly	flies in a rocket	_____
my shorts	a cup of tea	_____
you drive a car	like to eat bones	_____
an astronaut	fluttered its wings	_____
dogs	on the road	_____

Unit 8: The *ar* letter pattern

Remember

The letters **ar** often **come together** in words.
It is a common **letter pattern**.

a ca**r**

a ca**r**d

Have a go

1 Add **ar** to the end of each word. Read the words you make.

a	b	c	d	e	f
c**ar**	b____	f____	j____	t____	st____
___car	_____	_____	_____	_____	_____

2 Read the words. Underline the **ar** in each word:

dark	harm	part	shark
charm	party	smart	farm
spark	bark	chart	alarm
park	cart	lark	dart

3 Write the words from question 2 in this chart:

arm words	**ark** words	**art** words

Remember

Compound words are made up of **two smaller words joined together**.

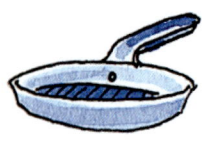      

pan   +   cake   =   pancake

Have a go

1 Do these word sums. Write the compound words you make.

a farm + yard = _____   b sea + side = _____

c bath + room = _____   d sheep + dog = _____

e sun + shine = _____   f snow + man = _____

g key + hole = _____   h run + way = _____

2 Write the correct compound word under each picture.

a  _____	b  _____	c  _____	d  _____
e  _____	f  _____	g  _____	h  _____

Unit 10: Checking up on verbs

Remember

Doing words are called **verbs**.
A **verb** tells us what someone or something is **doing**.

A snake **slithers** through the grass.

Have a go

1 Write the correct verb in each gap.

comb	read	bang	sing	tie	eat

a You _____ a book.

b You _____ a song.

c You _____ a knot.

d You _____ your hair.

e You _____ a sandwich.

f You _____ a drum.

2 Fill each gap with a suitable verb.

a You c _____ a ladder.

b You p _____ a picture.

c You r _____ a bike.

d You m _____ the grass.

e You c _____ a ball.

f You s _____ in a bed.

Unit 11: Opposite meanings

 **Remember**

Antonyms are words which mean the **opposite**.

hot   cold

 **Have a go**

Match up the pairs of opposites.

Write the words here.

fast	happy
hot	far
sad	slow
open	quiet
noisy	cold
near	shut
weak	dry
heavy	strong
fat	short
long	thin
wet	light

_____

_____

fast   slow

_____

_____

_____

_____

_____

_____

_____

Unit 12: Spelling and writing *th* words

Remember

When the letters **th** come together in a word, they make **one** sound.

To make the **th** sound, put your tongue between your front teeth and blow!

thief

Have a go

1 Complete each word with **th**. Read the words you make.

a **th**in	b clo____	c ____ing	d too____	e pa____
_thin_____	_____	_____	_____	_____

f ____ick	g ____ank	h ba____	i ____ink	j bo____
_____	_____	_____	_____	_____

2 Write the words you made in this chart:

words beginning with **th**	words ending with **th**

3 Write the **th** word that rhymes with:

a wing _____   b wink _____

c moth _____   d bin _____

e bank _____   f wick _____

15

Unit 13: Singular and plural

Remember

A noun may be either **singular** or **plural**.
Singular means **one** thing. Plural means **more than one** thing.
We just **add s** to the **end** of many nouns to make them plural.

one rabbit

lots of rabbit**s**

Have a go

1 Add **s** to each singular noun to make it plural.
   One has been done for you.

singular	plural
one shoe	lots of **shoes**
one book	lots of _____
one coat	lots of _____
one shirt	lots of _____
one cap	lots of _____
one dog	lots of _____

2 Rewrite each sentence correctly.

The underlined noun in each sentence is wrong.

a There were lots of <u>cow</u> in the field. _____

b I picked up a <u>cakes</u> and ate it. _____

c Some <u>lion</u> roar loudly. _____

d All the <u>duck</u> were on the pond. _____

e One <u>squirrels</u> was looking for a nut. _____

f Lots of <u>girl</u> were riding their bikes. _____

Unit 14: Using commas in lists

Remember

Commas are used to **separate** things in a **list**.

mouse, hamster, gerbil, guinea pig

Have a go

1 Put in the missing commas in these lists.

a orange blue red green yellow

b horse cow goat sheep hen

c curry spaghetti pizza hamburger sausages

d guitar drums piano trumpet trombone

e hammer chisel saw screwdriver drill

f shirt trousers socks shorts tie

2 List the names of these animals in **alphabetical order**. Don't forget the commas!

a camel alligator deer bear

_____

b goat elephant fox horse

_____

c panda kangaroo ostrich jaguar monkey

_____

d tiger wolf rabbit yak sheep

_____

e ox hedgehog panther lion duck

_____

Remember

When you say longer words **slowly** you can hear how they can be **broken down into smaller parts**. These parts are called **syllables**.

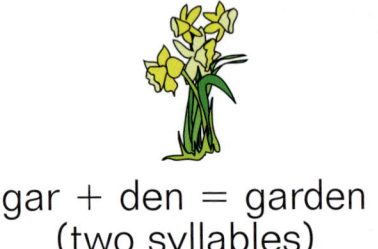

gar + den = garden
(two syllables)

Tap out the syllables when you say each word.

Have a go

1 Do these syllable sums. Each word has two syllables.

a car + pet = __carpet__   b hap + py = _____

c rab + bit = _____   d mag + net = _____

e help + ful = _____   f cab + bage = _____

g sing + ing = _____   h an + gry = _____

i tur + key = _____   j ro + bot = _____

2 Use the words with two syllables to label the pictures.

a	b	c	d	e
_____	_____	_____	_____	_____

f	g	h	i	j
_____	_____	_____	_____	_____

Remember

Always look carefully at words to see if you can spot any **common letter patterns**.

a h**are** with a squ**are**

a girl with f**air** h**air**

Have a go

1 Make these words. Read the words you make.

a	b	c	d
sh are	c are	s c are	s t are
share	_____	_____	_____

2 Write the correct word from question 1 under each picture.

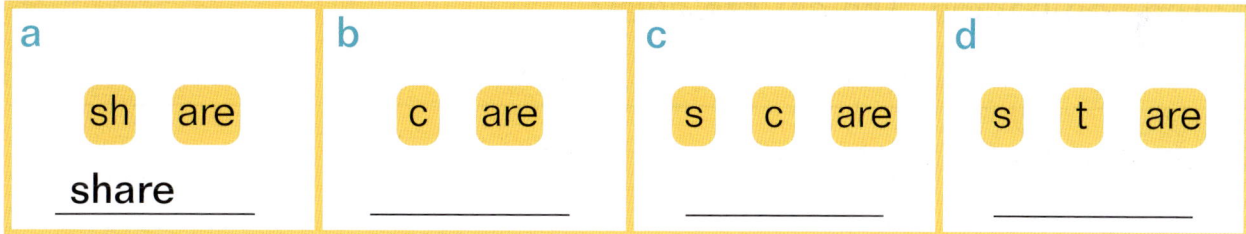

a _____ care   b _____   c _____   d _____

3 Complete each word with **air**. Read the words you make.

a	b	c	d
ch_____	p_____	h_____	f_____y

4 Write the correct word from question 3 under each picture.

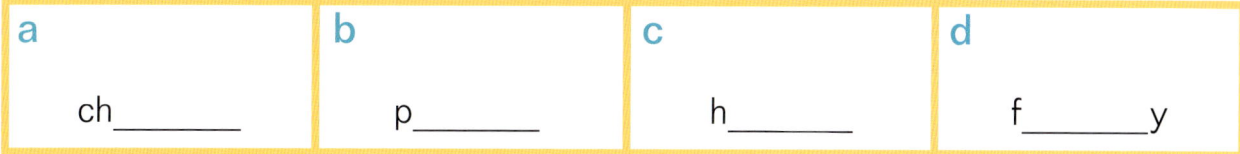

      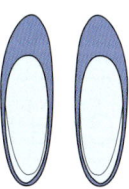

a _____   b _____   c _____   d _____

Unit 17: Joining sentences with *and*

Remember

A **conjunction** is a **joining** word. We use a **conjunction** to join two short sentences together to make one longer sentence.

I got up. I got dressed.

I got up **and** I got dressed.

Write each pair of sentences as one long sentence.
Join them with the conjunction **and**.

a The dog barked. The cat ran away.

_____

b I picked up my book. I read it.

_____

c I dropped the ball. It bounced in the road.

_____

d Mr Shah opened the garage. He got his car out.

_____

e There are no clouds in the sky. The sun is shining.

_____

f I went to the shop. I bought some sweets.

_____

g The bird flew down. It caught a worm.

_____

h Cara has dark hair. She has brown eyes.

_____

Unit 18: Using exclamation marks

Remember

We use an **exclamation mark** when we **feel strongly** about something.

Stop shouting**!**

Have a go

1 Tick ☑ the sentences that end with exclamation marks.

a Get me out of here! ☐   b Where are you? ☐   c It is raining. ☐

d How nice to see you! ☐   e I love ice creams! ☐   f Did you call me? ☐

g There are six pencils. ☐   h Stop pushing me! ☐   i Can you do it? ☐

j Help! I'm stuck! ☐   k What a horrible day! ☐   l It is Saturday. ☐

2 Read each sentence. Rewrite each exclamation correctly. Put in the capital letters and exclamation marks.

a come here at once _____

b stop annoying me _____

c don't do that _____

d what a lovely picture _____

e it's not fair _____

f this is terrible _____

g what a sensible child you are _____

h be quiet _____

Remember

Synonyms are words that have **similar meanings**.

happy   cheerful

Have a go

Match up the pairs of synonyms.

	Write the words here.

sad	quick
frightened	small
fast	unhappy
wet	huge
tiny	damp
big	stop
start	difficult
hard	begin
end	scared

Write the words here.
↓

_____

_____

_sad   unhappy_____

_____

_____

_____

_____

_____

_____

Remember

Sometimes we use **speech bubbles** to show someone is speaking. The **words the person says** go **inside** the speech bubbles.

What's for dinner?

You can have fish fingers or pizza.

Have a go

I like books.

I like to play.

I like my trainers.

Vicky

Rehannah

Jack

I like cats.

I like my computer games.

I like playing football.

Claire

Alex

Toby

Write what each of these children said:

a Alex: _____

b Vicky: _____

c Jack: _____

d Toby: _____

e Rehannah: _____

f Claire: _____

Test 1

Check how much you have learned.

Answer the questions.
Mark your answers. Fill in your score.

SCORE

1 Fill in the missing vowel in each word.

a  b

c___t   d___ck

out of 2

2 Do these word sums. Write the words you make.

a **p** + **e** + **n** = _____   b **h** + **o** + **t** = _____

out of 2

3 Underline the two words that rhyme.

pin   ten   win

out of 2

4 Circle the best ending for each sentence.

a flower.

a The girl climbed

a tree.

a balloon.

b The boy popped

a bat.

out of 2

5 Write these sentences correctly.

a it rained a lot

_____

b we got very wet

_____

6 Fill each gap with the correct noun.

clock   book

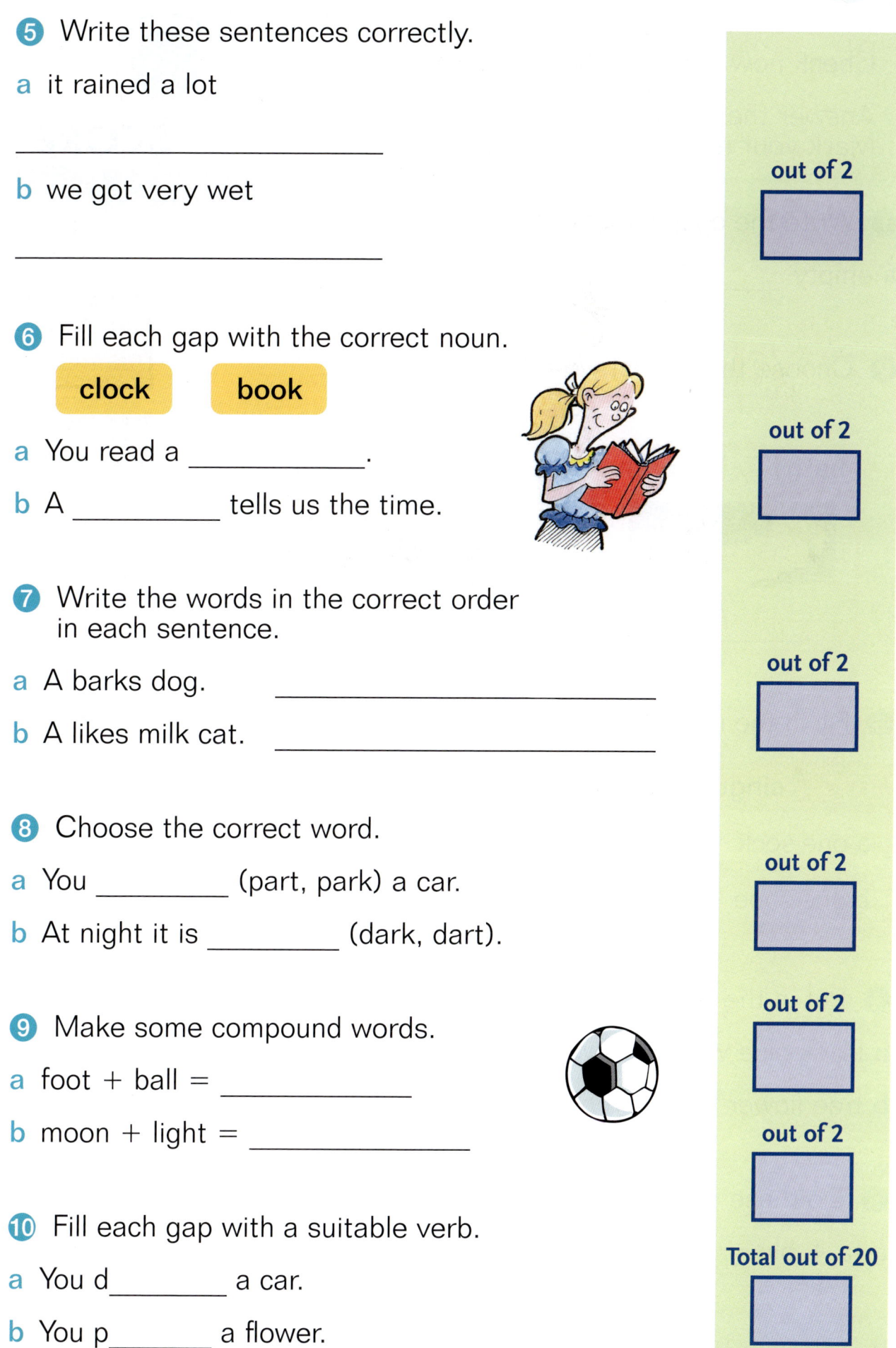

a You read a _____.

b A _____ tells us the time.

7 Write the words in the correct order
   in each sentence.

a A barks dog.   _____

b A likes milk cat.   _____

8 Choose the correct word.

a You _____ (part, park) a car.

b At night it is _____ (dark, dart).

9 Make some compound words.

a foot + ball = _____

b moon + light = _____

10 Fill each gap with a suitable verb.

a You d_____ a car.

b You p_____ a flower.

Test 2

Check how much you have learned.

Answer the questions.
Mark your answers. Fill in your score.

1 Write the opposite of:

a empty _____

b heavy _____

2 Choose the correct word for each picture.

a

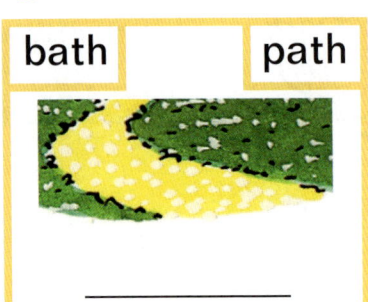

| bath | path |

_____

b

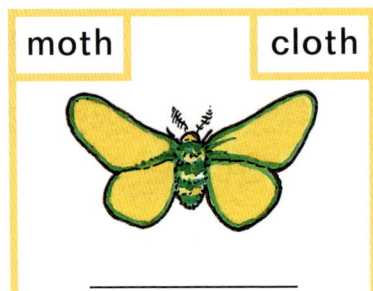

| moth | cloth |

_____

3 Fill in the missing words.

singular	plural
a one sock	two _____
b one shoe	two _____

4 Put in the missing commas.

a black blue white yellow

b tree flower bush shrub

5 Do these syllable sums:

a ta + ble = _____   b set + tee = _____

6 Choose **are** or **air** to fill each gap.

a ch_____

b squ_____

7 Write each pair of sentences as one long sentence.
Join them with the conjunction **and**.

a It is raining. It is cold.

_____

b I went home. I had my tea.

_____

out of 2

8 Write each exclamation correctly.

a it isn't fair   _____

b this is wonderful   _____

out of 2

9 Underline the pair of synonyms.

tiny   sharp   small

out of 2

10 Write each sentence in the correct speech bubble.

I make bread.   I mend cars.

a   b

out of 2

Total out of 20

Parents' notes

Unit 1: Vowels and consonants   The letters of the alphabet may be divided into vowels and consonants. There are five vowels – **a**, **e**, **i**, **o** and **u**. All the other letters are consonants. Every word must have at least one vowel in it. (Note that the letter **y** sometimes acts as a part-time vowel in words like 'my'.)

Unit 2: Making words with phonemes   All words are made up of phonemes (units of sound). Sometimes phonemes may be single letters. Sometimes they consist of two or more letters which make one sound e.g. **ea**. Your child needs to know how to build up words using phonemes. In this unit single-letter phonemes are used.

Unit 3: Rhyming words   Rhyming involves good listening skills. The ability to differentiate and hear differences in sounds and rhymes is an important early reading and spelling skill. In this unit the rhyming parts of the pairs of words sound and look similar.

Unit 4: Writing sensible sentences   Remind your child that all sentences they read or write should make sense. This activity involves choosing the most sensible ending for each sentence from the two alternatives given.

Unit 5: Capital letters and full stops   All sentences should begin with a capital letter. Most sentences end with a full stop. (Note that questions and exclamations do not.) The full stop is an important sign to the reader. It helps break up the text into meaningful units, and it indicates when to take a pause.

Unit 6: Checking up on nouns   All words may be classified according to the jobs they do in sentences. Nouns (naming words) play an essential part in grammar.

Unit 7: Sentences   We make sentences by putting words in order. The order we arrange the words in can make a lot of difference! It is always a good idea to get your child to read through a finished piece of work to check that each sentence he or she has written makes sense.

Unit 8: The *ar* letter pattern   There are many common letter patterns (letters which frequently come together) in words. It is important for your child to recognise these when reading and to be able to use them when writing. The letter pattern **ar** is the focus of this unit.

Unit 9: Making compound words   Compound words are words that are made by joining two smaller words together to make one longer word. A useful spelling strategy to learn is to look for smaller words 'hiding' inside longer words.

Unit 10: Checking up on verbs   All words may be classified according to the jobs they do in sentences. Verbs (doing words) play an essential part in grammar.

Unit 11: Opposite meanings   Antonyms are words whose meanings are as different as possible from each other i.e. opposites.

Unit 12: Spelling and writing *th* words   The phoneme **th** is the focus of this unit. Whenever the letters **th** come together your child needs to know that they are not sounded separately, but make one sound.

Unit 13: Singular and plural   Remind your child that many words may be extended by adding suffixes (word endings). In this unit turning single nouns into their plural form by adding **s** is studied (e.g. one car but two car**s**).

Unit 14: Using commas in lists   We use commas to separate items in a list. Commas are a signal to the reader to pause briefly.

Unit 15: Understanding syllables   When we say words slowly we can hear how they may be broken down into smaller parts, called syllables. It is helpful to tap or clap these 'beats' when saying words to stress the syllables. Another way is to get your child to say the words like a robot or Dalek!

Unit 16: Looking at *are* and *air*   It is important to get your child to look carefully at groups of words to try to spot any common letter patterns (letters which frequently come together) in them. These are often important as 'building blocks' for reading and writing. The letter patterns **are** (as in 'square') and **air** (as in 'chair') are the focus of this unit.

Unit 17: Joining sentences with *and*   A conjunction is a joining word which may be used to join two sentences together. The most common conjunction is the word **and**. In order to get your child to understand this idea, it is helpful to think of a road junction where two roads meet.

Unit 18: Using exclamation marks   An exclamation mark is a signal to the reader. An exclamation mark is used at the end of a sentence to show strong feelings about something.

Unit 19: Words with similar meanings   Synonyms are words which have the same, or very similar, meanings. Using synonyms makes our writing more interesting and adds variety. Encourage your child to use a thesaurus if you have one.

Unit 20: Using speech bubbles   Your child will be familiar with the concept of speech bubbles through picture books and comics. Remind your child that all the words the person actually says go inside the speech bubble itself.

Answers

Unit 1: Vowels and consonants (page 4)

1 h<u>a</u>t, b<u>e</u>d, p<u>i</u>n, c<u>o</u>t, b<u>u</u>t, s<u>i</u>p, f<u>a</u>t, s<u>u</u>n, g<u>e</u>t, p<u>o</u>t, h<u>u</u>g, n<u>e</u>t, l<u>a</u>p, f<u>o</u>g, b<u>i</u>n.

2 a frog   b drum   c sack   d leg
   e kiss   f rug   g hill   h nest
   i map   j bag

Unit 2: Making words with phonemes (page 5)

1 a map b hen c six d cot e hut
   f zip g peg h cap i log j mug

2 a cot b map c hut d six e hen
   f zip g log h cap i peg j mug

Unit 3: Rhyming words (page 6)

stay	tray	lost	cost
hill	fill	meet	greet
lick	stick	bite	white
slow	throw	moan	groan
cry	try	rain	drain

Unit 4: Writing sensible sentences (page 7)

a A car has four wheels.
b The mouse squeaked.
c Tom drank a cup of tea.
d The girl read the book.
e A squirrel ran up the tree.
f An apple has lots of pips.
g The lion roared.

Unit 5: Capital letters and full stops (page 8)

a Claire ran home from school.
b She felt very hungry.
c Claire went into the kitchen.
d She made some cheese sandwiches.
e Then she put some cakes on the table.
f Next Claire put some crisps in a dish.
g After this she made a drink.
h When everything was ready Claire had her tea.

Unit 6: Checking up on nouns (page 9)

1 a boat b ambulance c aeroplane
   d fire engine e submarine f train

2 a school   b hammer   c tap
   d money   e knife   f window

Unit 7: Sentences (page 10)

1 Sharks swim.   Horses gallop.
   Snakes slither.   Frogs hop.
   Birds fly.   Butterflies flutter.

2 You drink a cup of tea.
   The butterfly fluttered its wings.
   My shorts are very muddy.
   You drive a car on the road.
   An astronaut flies in a rocket.
   Dogs like to eat bones.

Unit 8: The *ar* letter pattern (page 11)

1 a car   b bar   c far   d jar
   e tar   f star

2 d<u>ar</u>k, h<u>ar</u>m, p<u>ar</u>t, sh<u>ar</u>k, ch<u>ar</u>m, p<u>ar</u>ty, sm<u>ar</u>t, f<u>ar</u>m, sp<u>ar</u>k, b<u>ar</u>k, ch<u>ar</u>t, al<u>ar</u>m, p<u>ar</u>k, c<u>ar</u>t, l<u>ar</u>k, d<u>ar</u>t

3

arm words	ark words	art words
harm	dark	part
charm	shark	party
farm	spark	smart
alarm	bark	chart
	park	cart
	lark	dart

Unit 9: Making compound words (page 12)

1 a farmyard   b seaside
   c bathroom   d sheepdog
   e sunshine   f snowman
   g keyhole   h runway

2 a seaside   b keyhole
   c snowman   d runway
   e farmyard   f bathroom
   g sheepdog   h sunshine

Unit 10: Checking up on verbs (page 13)

1 a read b sing c tie d comb
   e eat f bang

2 a climb b paint c ride d mow
   e catch f sleep

Unit 11: Opposite meanings (page 14)

sad   happy   near   far
fast   slow   noisy   quiet
hot   cold   open   shut
wet   dry   weak   strong
long   short   fat   thin
heavy   light

Unit 12: Spelling and writing *th* words (page 15)

1 a thin b cloth c thing d tooth
   e path f thick g thank h bath
   i think j both

2

words beginning with **th**	words ending with **th**
thin	cloth
thing	tooth
thick	path
thank	bath
think	both

3 a thing b think c cloth d thin
   e thank f thick

Unit 13: Singular and plural (page 16)

1

singular	plural
one shoe	lots of shoes
one book	lots of **books**
one coat	lots of **coats**
one shirt	lots of **shirts**
one cap	lots of **caps**
one dog	lots of **dogs**

2 a There were lots of cows in the field.

b I picked up a cake and ate it.
c Some lions roar loudly.
d All the ducks were on the pond.
e One squirrel was looking for a nut.
f Lots of girls were riding their bikes.

Unit 14: Using commas in lists (page 17)

1 a orange, blue, red, green, yellow
   b horse, cow, goat, sheep, hen
   c curry, spaghetti, pizza, hamburger, sausages
   d guitar, drums, piano, trumpet, trombone
   e hammer, chisel, saw, screwdriver, drill
   f shirt, trousers, socks, shorts, tie

2 a alligator, bear, camel, deer
   b elephant, fox, goat, horse
   c jaguar, kangaroo, monkey, ostrich, panda
   d rabbit, sheep, tiger, wolf, yak
   e duck, hedgehog, lion, ox, panther

Unit 15: Understanding syllables (page 18)

1 a carpet b happy c rabbit
   d magnet e helpful f cabbage
   g singing h angry i turkey
   j robot

2 a magnet b rabbit c robot
   d carpet e singing f cabbage
   g angry h turkey i happy
   j helpful

Unit 16: Looking at *are* and *air* (page 19)

1 a share b care c scare d stare

2 a care b share c stare d scare

3 a chair b pair c hair d fairy

4 a hair b chair c fairy d pair

Unit 17: Joining sentences with *and* (page 20)

a The dog barked **and** the cat ran away.
b I picked up my book **and** I read it.
c I dropped the ball **and** it bounced in the road.
d Mr Shah opened the garage **and** he got his car out.
e There are no clouds in the sky **and** the sun is shining.
f I went to the shop **and** I bought some sweets.
g The bird flew down **and** it caught a worm.
h Cara has dark hair **and** she has brown eyes.

Unit 18: Using exclamation marks (page 21)

1 a Get me out of here! ✓
b Where are you?
c It is raining.
d How nice to see you! ✓
e I love ice creams!   ✓
f Did you call me?
g There are six pencils.
h Stop pushing me!   ✓
i Can you do it?
j Help! I'm stuck!   ✓
k What a horrible day! ✓
l It is Saturday.

2 a Come here at once!
b Stop annoying me!
c Don't do that!
d What a lovely picture!
e It's not fair!
f This is terrible!
g What a sensible child you are!
h Be quiet!

Unit 19: Words with similar meanings (page 22)

fast	quick	tiny	small
sad	unhappy	big	huge
wet	damp	end	stop
hard	difficult	start	begin
frightened	scared		

Unit 20: Using speech bubbles (page 23)

a Alex: I like my computer games.
b Vicky: I like books.
c Jack: I like my trainers.
d Toby: I like playing football.
e Rehannah: I like to play.
f Claire: I like cats.

Test 1 (pages 24 and 25)

1 a c**a**t   b d**u**ck

2 a pen   b hot

3 pin   win

4 a The girl climbed a tree.
b The boy popped a balloon.

5 a It rained a lot.
b We got very wet.

6 a book   b clock

7 a A dog barks. b A cat likes milk.

8 a park   b dark

9 a football b moonlight

10 a drive   b pick/plant

Test 2 (pages 26 and 27)

1 a full   b light

2 a path   b moth

3 a socks   b shoes

4 a black, blue, white, yellow
b tree, flower, bush, shrub

5 a table   b settee

6 a chair   b squ**are**

7 a It is raining and it is cold.
b I went home and I had my tea.

8 a It isn't fair! b This is wonderful!

9 tiny   small

10 a I mend cars. b I make bread.